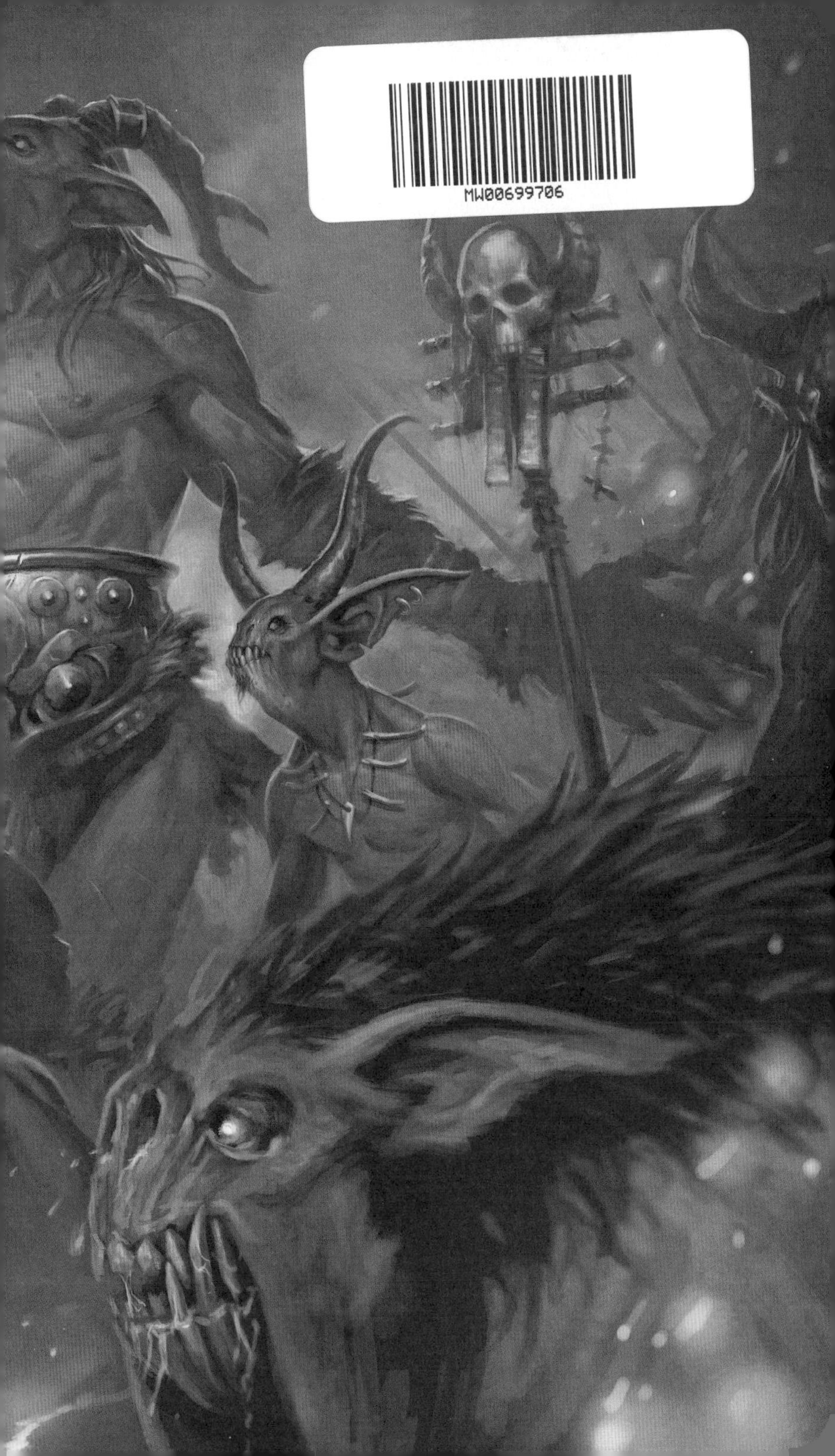

PROPERTY OF: